DMAIC

Project Execution Essentials Handbook

Sumeet Savant

Dedication

To all Lean Six Sigma enthusiasts and practitioners.

Contents

Acknowledgment

Special thanks to my wife Sahana, for always supporting me in all my endeavors and to the exciting world of Lean Six Sigma for accepting me and providing me a platform to perform on a global scale.

About the Author

Sumeet Savant is a Lean Six Sigma Master Black Belt Mentor and Coach, with more than a decade of experience in executing, leading and mentoring Lean Six Sigma process improvement projects. He is a BTech, MBA, and Prince certified Practitioner. He has facilitated hundreds of process improvement projects, and coached hundreds of professionals, Yellow, Green, and Black Belts over the years. He lives in Mumbai, India with his family.

Lean Six Sigma Project Execution Essentials Series

Handbooks that will help you execute a variety of Lean Six Sigma projects,

◆ Plan Do Check Act
◆ DMAIC
◆ DMADV
◆ DMADOV
◆ Lean Action Workout
◆ Lean DMAIC
◆ Lean DMADV
◆ Lean DMADOV

Purpose of writing this book

With businesses around the world focusing on delivering value to their customer, the goal of process improvements and value additions have flown down to each and every individual employee working for the organization. As a result, not only the organization's success, but also the individual's success in terms of growth today heavily depend upon the value they deliver and the improvements they implement in the processes and products for the customer.

Today employees know that they need to deliver value, however due to the already tight deadlines they are expected to meet and their ever-increasing workload, their focus towards improvement projects and value additions tend to take a lower priority. This is especially true as the quality of the documentation required to execute process improvements in the form of six sigma projects, lean projects and PDCA projects is much high. And many times, they are unclear as what exactly should the content of the documents be.

This impacts their individual contribution towards process improvements, and hence their growth, which in turn also impacts the overall business growth.

DMAIC is a Six Sigma improvement cycle, driven by data, used for improving business processes and products.

This book is aimed at enabling businesses and their employees execute DMAIC projects seamlessly and effectively, focusing only on the critical components, which will ensure a successful DMAIC project execution.

What this book aims to help you with

This book aims to help you with the following,

◆ Explain the core essential components needed to execute a DMAIC project.

◆ Explain how to execute a DMAIC project, using the core essential components.

◆ Cover the above in least number of words possible – to help you deliver a DMAIC faster.

However, please note that this book does not aim to,

✗ Make you an expert in the DMAIC – your organization expects you to deliver DMAIC projects faster, so we will keep our focus to that.

DMAIC

DMAIC, one of the most famous Six Sigma frameworks, is a methodology, used when an existing process or product needs to be improved further to meet customer specifications. It focuses primarily on improving and optimizing an existing process or product and consists of five phases.

DEFINE – Involves defining the business problem, goal, team, scope and the project timelines.

MEASURE – Involves establishing process performance baselines, or the current performance of the process or product.

ANALYZE – Involves analyzing, identifying, and selecting the root causes behind the problem.

IMPROVE - Involves identifying, testing and implementing a solution for the problem.

CONTROL - Involves measuring and monitoring the improvements to ensure controlled and sustained success.

DMAIC – The Essential Components

The essential components of a DMAIC project are,

DEFINE
◆ Charter
◇ Business Case
◇ Problem Statement
◇ Goal Statement
◇ Scope
◇ Project Team
◇ Time-lines
◆ Critical To Quality
◆ SIPOC

MEASURE
◆ Measurement System Analysis
◆ Performance Standards
◆ AS IS Data

ANALYZE
◆ AS IS Process Capability
◆ Root Cause Analysis

IMPROVE
◆ Solution Identification
◆ Verification and Validation

CONTROL
◆ TO BE Data
◆ TO BE Process Capability
◆ Data Review
◆ Monitor and Control Plan
◆ Realization, Communication and Signoff

DEFINE Essential Components

The essential components of a Define phase are,

◆ Charter
◇ Business Case
◇ Problem Statement
◇ Goal Statement
◇ Scope
◇ Project Team
◇ Time-lines

◆ Critical to Quality

◆ SIPOC

Charter - What and Why

◆ What it is

A concise document that clearly describes the elements
of the project by explaining the Business Case, the
Problem, the Goal, the Scope, the Team and the
Timelines of a project.

◆ Why is it important

This is the most important component as it acts as a
reference and a guide to manage and take the project to
success.

Charter - How to Frame

◆ **Frame the Charter** by including the following components,

◇ Business Case
  ◇ Problem Statement
  ◇ Goal Statement
  ◇ Scope
  ◇ Project Team
  ◇ Time-lines

Business Case - What and Why

◆ What it is

A concise description of the improvement opportunity, explaining in brief the problem, the goal of the project, the reason why the project is important, along with financial justification if any for the execution of the project, and most importantly what is the negative impact, if the project is not executed right now.

◆ Why is it important

This is the most important component as it enables the sponsor of the project to decide whether he can approve the particular opportunity for execution, over other potential improvement opportunities.

Business Case - How to Frame

◆ **Frame the Business Case** with a view to answer the following questions,

◇ What is the problem, the DMAIC project is trying to solve or improve, what is the business opportunity?
◇ Where and with what frequency is the problem occurring?
◇ What is the financial impact of the problem?
◇ What is the business value of executing the DMAIC project?
◇ What is the impact or risk of not utilizing the business opportunity right now?

Take approval from sponsor on the Business Case before you proceed.

Business Case - Points to note

◆ **Points to note while framing the Business Case**

◇ Avoid mentioning the solution in the Business Case.

◇ Avoid giving any hint towards the solution in the Business Case.

◇ Avoid having exact same text in the Business Cases as in Problem and Goal statements; though they are related, they are not same.

◇ Ensure the impact of not executing the DMAIC project right now, is mentioned.

◇ Ensure financial benefits of executing the project is mentioned in the Business Case.

Business Case - Example

◆ **Business Case:**

"ABC Business's XYZ Support Team performs daily monitoring, reporting user activity on XYZ system.

The report captures the details of daily active users on the XYZ system, including their ID, name, 'Last Activity Date' and 'Role'.

☐ The XYZ support team fetches details required for the report.
☐ Creates an excel report.
☐ And sends to the Business lead.

Daily there are at least around 50 active users for whom the data needs to be fetched.

Fetching the details, formatting the data into an excel report, and sending to the Business Lead takes around 2 hours daily, amounting to 47,450 USD annually.

This project aims at reducing this manual effort wastage by at least 80% and achieving a dollar saving of at least 37960 USD.

If this project is not initiated right now, it will result in continued wastage of effort and productivity"

Problem Statement - What and Why

◆ What it is

A concise description of the problem or the issue or the condition which the DMAIC project focuses to improve.

◆ Why is it important

This is an important component as it helps identify the gap between the current and desired states of a process or product. This basically helps the team understand why the DMAIC project is being done.

Problem Statement - How to Frame

◆ **Frame the Problem Statement** with a view to answer the following questions related to the problem, the DMAIC project is trying to fix or improve,

◇ What is the problem the DMAIC project is trying to solve or improve?

◇ Where is the problem occurring?

◇ When does the problem occur and with what frequency?

◇ What is the financial impact of the problem?

Problem Statement - Points to note

◆ Points to note while framing the Problem Statement

◇ Avoid mentioning the solution in the Problem Statement.

◇ Avoid giving any hint towards the solution in the Problem Statement.

◇ Avoid having exact same text in the Business Cases as in Problem and Goal statements; though they are related, they are not same.

◇ Ensure financial impact of the problem is mentioned in the Problem Statement.

◇ Usually the Problem statement will have a more detailed description of the problem than the Business Case.

Problem Statement - Example

◆ Problem Statement:

"ABC Business's XYZ Support Team performs daily monitoring, reporting user activity on XYZ system.

The report captures the details of daily active users on the XYZ system, including their ID, name, 'Last Activity Date' and 'Role'.

☐ The XYZ support team fetches the users active within the last 24 hour, along with their 'ID', and 'Name' from the XYZ system log database.
☐ Then it fetches 'Last Activity Date' for all these active users from XYZ system.
☐ And 'Role' from the company employee data source.
☐ The XYZ team then puts the data into an excel file, formats it.
☐ And then emails this excel report to the Business Lead.

Daily there are around 50 active users for whom the data needs to be fetched.

Fetching the details from multiple sources and formatting the data into an excel takes around 2 hours daily.

This amounts to 47,450 USD annually at 65 USD hourly rate, and is a huge expense and productivity loss."

Goal Statement - What and Why

◆ What it is

A concise description of the goal or the aim or the desired state which the DMAIC project focuses to achieve within a specified period of time.

◆ Why is it important

This is an important component as it helps identify the desired state of a process or product. It also helps identify the improvement target, and the deadline for the project.

Goal Statement - How to Frame

◆ **Frame the Goal Statement** with a view to answer the following questions related to the aim of the DMAIC project,

◇ What is the DMAIC project targeting to improve?
◇ By how much percent is the DMAIC project targeting to improve, that what it aims to improve?
◇ By when is the DMAIC project targeting to improve, that what it aims to improve?
◇ What would the financial benefits be?

Overall the goal statement needs to be SMART (Specific, Measurable, Attainable, Relevant, Timebound)

Goal Statement - Points to note

◆ **Points to note while framing the Goal Statement**

◇ Start with a verb.
◇ Ensure to mention what the project aims to improve.
◇ Ensure to include the target in terms of percentage improvement.
◇ Ensure the time line is mentioned.

Goal Statement - Example

◆ **Goal Statement:**

"Reduce the manual effort spent creating the daily activity monitor report by at least 80% by 30th June 2018, resulting in annual saving of at least 37960 USD"

Scope - What and Why

◆ What it is

A concise description clearly demarcating what is in
scope and what is out of scope of the DMAIC project.

◆ Why is it important

This is an important component as it helps to keep the
team focused, and to set clear expectations for the
stakeholders.

Scope - How to Frame

◆ **Frame the Scope** with a view to answer the following questions for the DMAIC project,

◇ What is in scope for the DMAIC project?
◇ What is NOT in scope for the DMAIC project?

Following are some of the things that can be scoped,

◇ Users
◇ Geographies
◇ Sub businesses
◇ Product features
◇ Time

Following are some of the ways to scope,

- ◇ Includes/Excludes
- ◇ SIPOC
- ◇ In Frame/ Out Frame
- ◇ Statement of Scope
- ◇ Work Breakdown Structure

Scope - Points to note

◆ Points to note while framing the Scope

◇ Sometimes it is enough to only include the In-scope, as anything out of In-scope will anyway be considered out of scope.

Scope - Example

◆ **Scope:** Includes Excludes Table

	Includes	Excludes
What	Daily XYZ Activity Monitoring Report	Any Other Report
Where	XYZ System	Any Other System
When	Daily	Any Other Frequency
Who	XYZ Team sends to Business Lead	Any Other Team

Project Team - What and Why

◆ What it is

A concise description clearly mentioning the roles, and names of the people involved and necessary for the successful execution of the DMAIC project.

◆ Why is it important

This is an important component as it helps define the project team, their roles, and any other important stakeholders.

Project Team - How to Frame

◆ **Frame the Project Team** with a view to answer the following questions related to the people, involved in the DMAIC project,

◇ Who are the people involved in the DMAIC project?
◇ What are the roles they are playing?

Following are some of the things that can be covered,

◇ Mentors
◇ Sponsor
◇ Project Lead
◇ Development Team
◇ Testing Team
◇ Deployment Team

Project Team - Points to note

◆ Points to note while framing the Project Team

◇ Do remember to mention the Sponsor.
◇ Projects normally have BB mentor and MBB mentor, ensure to mention them.
◇ Sometimes there is an alternate lead along with the primary lead, mention them both.
◇ Capture details of any other important stakeholders.

Project Team - Example

◆ **Project Team:**

◇ GB: Maruti M
◇ BB: Shani M
◇ Sponsor: Neelkanth S
◇ MBB: Sumeet Savant

Time-lines - What and Why

◆ **What it is**

A concise description clearly mentioning the time-lines needed for completion of the entire project, as well as for each phase of the DMAIC project.

◆ **Why is it important**

This is an important component as it helps keep the team focused, and to set clear expectations for the stakeholders.

Time-lines - How to Frame

◆ **Frame the Time-lines** with a view to answer the following questions related to the planned schedule of the DMAIC project,

◇ What are the time-lines for execution of each of the phase of the DMAIC project?

Following are some of the ways this can be presented,

◇ Activity Diagram
◇ Schedule Diagram
◇ Gant Chart
◇ Sequence Diagram
◇ Simple Table

Time-lines - Points to note

◆ **Points to note while framing the Time-lines**

◇ The time-lines need to stand out clearly for the phases.
◇ Care needs to be taken to ensure correct representations in case of diagrams.

Time-lines - Example

◆ **Time-lines:**

◇ DEFINE Start Date – 1st April 2018
◇ DEFINE End Date – 15th April 2018

◇ MEASURE Start Date – 16th April 2018
◇ MEASURE End Date – 30th April 2018

◇ ANALYZE Start Date – 1st May 2018
◇ ANALYZE End Date – 15th May 2018

◇ IMPROVE Start Date – 16th May 2018
◇ IMPROVE End Date – 31st May 2018

◇ CONTROL Start Date – 1st June 2018
◇ CONTROL End Date – 30th June 2018

Critical to Quality - What and Why

◆ What it is

A concise description describing what is Critical to Quality for the project, and the Y Metric, arising from the voice of customer.

◆ Why is it important

This is an important component as it helps to determine what is critical to quality for the DMAIC project to be successful, from customer point of view, and what will be measured to evaluate the same.

Critical to Quality - How to Frame

◆ **Frame the Critical To Quality** with a view to answer the following questions,

◇ What is the Voice of Customer?
◇ What are the key drivers or the CTQ?
◇ What will be measured for each of these drivers?

Draw the Critical To Quality tree to answer these questions.

Critical to Quality - Points to note

◆ Points to note while framing the Critical to Quality

◇ Be careful while establishing the drivers, these are the factors that customers should provide and agree to.

Critical to Quality - Example

◆ **Critical to Quality:**

◇ CTQ: Effort
◇ Y Metric: Effort to create the Daily report
◇ CTQ Tree Diagram

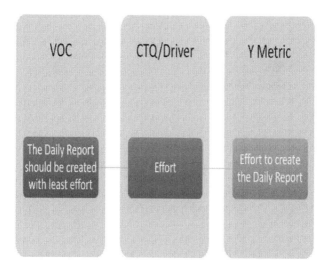

SIPOC - What and Why

◆ What it is

A concise description describing the high level map of the current process.

◆ Why is it important

This is an important component as it helps give a high level view and idea of the process to the team and stakeholders before going into in depth analysis.

SIPOC - How to Frame

◆ **Frame the SIPOC** with a view to answer the following questions,

◇ Who are the supplier to the process?
◇ What are the inputs the supplier provides, to be fed to the process?
◇ What arc the steps happening in the process, at a high level?
◇ What are the outputs of the process?
◇ Who are the customers or the recipients of the process?

To answer these questions, draw a high level map of the current process, and highlight the following,

Supplier - Someone or something that provides input to the process.

Input - Raw material that is fed to the process.

Process - Sequence of steps or activities that convert the input to output.

Output - Result of the process.

Customer - Recipient of the output.

SIPOC - Points to note

◆ **Points to note while framing the SIPOC**

◇ Identify the items correctly.
◇ Ensure there is clear demarcation between the I and O.
◇ Ensure there is clear demarcation between the S and C.
◇ Keep it simple and easy to understand.

SIPOC - Example

◆ **SIPOC:** SIPOC Diagram

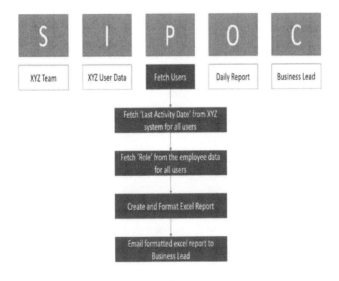

MEASURE Essential Components

The essential components of a Measure phase are,

◆ Measurement System Analysis

◆ Performance Standards

◆ AS IS Data

Measurement System Analysis - What and Why

◆ What it is

A concise description describing the details of the analysis, performed on the measurement system, to analyze the amount of variation introduced by the measurement system itself.

◆ Why is it important

This is an important component, as it helps to ensure that the collected data is accurate, by confirming that the measurement system itself does not introduce any variation or error of its own.

Measurement System Analysis - How to Frame

◆ **Frame the Measurement System Analysis** with a view to answer the following questions,

◇ What are the MSA Measures?
◇ What is the Assessment used?
◇ What is the data variation observed?
◇ If any action need to be taken in case variation is found?

Some of the most important measures to assess a measurement system are,

Repeatability – Ability of a measurement system to produce same values each and every time the same appraiser measures the same sample.

Reproducibility – Ability of a measurement system to produce same values every time a different appraiser measures the same sample.

Accuracy – Ability of a measurement system to produce values as close as possible to the correct value of the measurements.

The most common MSA technique used to assess Repeatability and Reproducibility is the Gauge RnR.

Measurement System Analysis - Points to note

◆ **Points to note while framing the Measurement System Analysis**

◇ Ensure there are enough data samples to perform MSA.

◇ Have two or more operators to participate in the MSA.

◇ Choose an appropriate method to perform the MSA.

◇ Avoid using fake data.

◇ Keep the number of samples or operators limited.

Measurement System Analysis - Example

◆ **Measurement System Analysis:**

◇ MSA Measures – Repeatability, Reproducibility
◇ Assessment used – Gage RnR
◇ Data variation observed – % RnR = 8.9%
◇ Any action taken in case variation was found – % RnR < 10% hence Measurement system is good.

Performance Standards - What and Why

◆ **What it is**

A concise description describing the performance level the customer expects from the process in terms of the CTQ and its metrics defined.

◆ **Why is it important**

This is an important component, as it helps to determine the levels of performance as expected by the customer, for the CTQ and Y Metric defined.

Performance Standards - How to Frame

◆ **Frame the Performance Standards** with a view to answer the following questions,

◇ What is the Critical to Quality (CTQ) from customer point of view?
◇ What is the Project Y Metric for the CTQ?
◇ What is the target - the performance expected?
◇ What are the tolerance levels?

Tabulate these details in a table for each CTQ.

Performance Standards - Points to note

◆ Points to note while framing the Performance Standards

◇ The Target performance is the level of performance the customer expects the process or product to deliver.

◇ Tolerance levels are the maximum and minimum levels of deviation the customer can afford to tolerate in the performance of the process or product.

◇ Lower Specification Level = Target - Tolerance.

◇ Upper Specification Level = Target + Tolerance.

◇ In DMAIC CTQ and Y Metric are determined in Define phase, and in Measure phase, the specifications or the performance standards are determined.

Performance Standards - Example

◆ **Performance Standards:** Performance Standards
Table

CTQ	Project Y Metric	Target	Tolerance
Effort	Effort to create the Daily Report in Minutes	20	+/- 4

AS IS Data - What and Why

◆ **What it is**

A concise description describing the performance of
the AS IS process derived from the data collected.

◆ **Why is it important**

This is an important component as it helps to
understand the current or AS IS performance.

AS IS Data - How to Frame

◆ **Frame the AS IS Data** with a view to answer the following questions,

◇ What is the performance of the current process, before implementing the solution?

Use appropriate sampling mechanism and collect a representative data sample from the data population.

Some of the common sampling techniques are,

◆ Probability Sampling
◇ Simple Random Sampling
◇ Stratified Sampling
◇ Cluster Sampling
◇ Systematic Sampling

- Non Probability Sampling
  - Volunteer Sampling
  - Haphazard Sampling

Some of the common data types are,

- Qualitative Data
  - Binary Data
  - Unordered Data
  - Ordered Data

- Quantitative Data
  - Continuous Data
  - Discrete Data

Tabulate the data collected.

AS IS Data - Points to note

◆ **Points to note while framing the AS IS Data**

◇ Choose appropriate sampling mechanism – sample should be representative of population.

◇ Choose appropriate data type.

◇ Avoid fake data, actually collect the data.

◇ Most importantly, clearly mention what is collected.

AS IS Data - Example

◆ **AS IS Data:** Effort in minutes to fetch data and prepare report manually (Mean) - 120 minutes

Reading No.	Effort in minutes to fetch data and prepare report
1	120
2	118
3	119
4	121
5	122
6	123
7	121
8	120
9	119
10	120
11	117
12	123
13	122
14	119
15	120
16	122
17	119
18	117
19	120
20	118
21	119
22	120
23	123
24	120
25	125

ANALYZE Essential Components

The essential components of a Analyze phase are,

◆ AS IS Process Capability

◆ Root Cause Analysis

AS IS Process Capability - What and Why

◆ **What it is**

A concise description describing the capability of the current or the AS IS process or product.

◆ **Why is it important**

This is an important component as it helps to determine the current process performance capability.

AS IS Process Capability - How to Frame

◆ **Frame the AS IS Process Capability** with a view to answer the following questions,

◇ What is the capability or the sigma value of the current process?

An online Sigma calculator can be used to calculate the process capability.

Following might be needed to calculate this,

◇ Mean
◇ Standard Deviation
◇ Specification Limits as defined by customer

AS IS Process Capability - Points to note

◆ Points to note while framing the AS IS Process Capability

◇ Ensure the right capability calculator is being used.

◇ Remember that Mean will be the mean of the AS IS collected data.

◇ Standard Deviation can be calculated for the collected data.

◇ Specification Limits can be calculated from goal statement target, or the CTQ performance requirements.

AS IS Process Capability - Example

◆ **AS IS Process Capability:**

◇ Mean - 120
◇ Standard Deviation - 1.9899748742132
◇ Specification Limits -
◇ LSL - 0
◇ USL - 24
◇ Potential Cp - 2.01
◇ Actual Cpk Index- (-)16.081

Root Cause Analysis - What and Why

◆ What it is

A concise description describing the root causes behind the problem in the process.

◆ Why is it important

This is an important component as it helps to exactly pinpoint contributing factors which will be worked upon and fixed to improve the process.

Root Cause Analysis - How to Frame

◆ **Frame the Root Cause Analysis** with a view to answer the following questions,

◇ What are the root causes behind the problems in the process, that the project is trying to improve?

Some of the tools that can be used are,

◇ The 5 Whys
◇ Brainstorming
◇ Fishbone or the Ishikawa Diagram
◇ Pareto Chart
◇ Run Chart
◇ Control Chart
◇ Histogram
◇ Scatter Diagram
◇ Flow Chart
◇ Design of Experiments

Root Cause Analysis - Points to note

◆ **Points to note while framing the Root Cause Analysis**

◇ Keep it concise, crisp, and simple.
◇ The Brainstorming, 5 whys and Fishbone Diagram are preferred tools.

Root Cause Analysis - Example

◆ **Root Cause Analysis:** 5 Why Root Cause Analysis revealed the root cause - Process not yet automated(Manual Process)

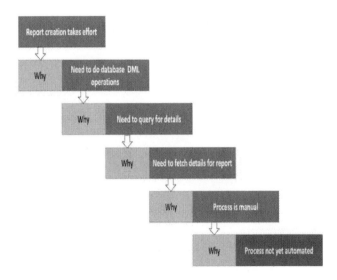

IMPROVE Essential Components

The essential components of a Improve phase are,

◆ Solution Identification

◆ Verification and Validation

Solution Identification - What and Why

◆ **What it is**

A concise description describing the probable solutions to fix the identified root causes. Followed by selection of one or more solution options to implement.

◆ **Why is it important**

This is an important component as it helps to determine the possible solutions and decide upon one or more solution to improve the process.

Solution Identification - How to Frame

◆ **Frame the Solution Identification** with a view to answer the following questions,

◇ What are the possible solutions for each of the identified root cause?

◇ Which is the best solution to choose and implement?

Some of the tools that can help select one or more solutions from a number of solutions are below,

◇ Solution Prioritization Matrix

◇ Criteria Based Matrix

◇ Pugh Matrix

Solution Identification - Points to note

◆ **Points to note while framing the Solution Identification**

◇ Try to keep things simple, and crisp.
◇ Analyze the options fairly, practically and without bias.
◇ The solution can be developed at this stage.

Solution Identification - Example

◆ **Solution Identification:** Solution Chosen using Criteria Based Matrix: Automate the manual process using java.

	Time to Implement 5	Complexity 4	Ease of Use 3	Total
Implement Solution Using Java	5	5	4	57
Implement Solution Using C	5	4	3	50
Implement Solution Using Python	2	4	2	32
Implement Solution Using PHP	3	3	4	39

Verification and Validation - What and Why

◆ **What it is**

A concise description describing the performed tests to verify and validate the correct working of the solution, along with the result.

◆ **Why is it important**

This is an important component as it helps to test the solution and confirm the correct working of the improved process.

Verification and Validation - How to Frame

◆ **Frame the Verification and Validation** with a view to answer the following questions,

◇ What are the tests performed to confirm the correct working of the improved process?
◇ What are the results of the testing?

Verification and Validation - Points to note

◆ **Points to note while framing the Verification and Validation**

◇ Ensure all necessary test cases are covered.
◇ Ensure all required and relevant testing is performed, we cannot move half tested product to production.
◇ Ensure signoff from appropriate users on testing.

Verification and Validation - Example

◆ **Verification and Validation:** Sample Unit Test Cases Result: Pass. Sign off on the testing – Signed off by business owner dated 16th June 2018.

Sl No.	Description	Expected Result	Observed Result
1	'Last Activity Date' from XYZ system, and 'Role' from the company employee data is fetched for the users	The details fetched should be accurate as present in the XYZ system and employee database	Same as Expected

CONTROL Essential Components

The essential components of a Control phase are,

◆ TO BE Data

◆ TO BE Process Capability

◆ Data Review

◆ Monitor and Control Plan

◆ Realization, Communication and Signoff

TO BE Data - What and Why

◆ **What it is**

A concise description describing the performance of
the TO BE process derived from the data collected.

◆ **Why is it important**

This is an important component as it helps to
understand the improved or the TO BE performance.

TO BE Data - How to Frame

◆ **Frame the TO BE Data** with a view to answer the following questions,

◇ What is the performance of the new process, after implementing the solution?

Use appropriate sampling mechanism and collect a representative data sample from the data population.

Some of the common sampling techniques are,

◆ Probability Sampling
◇ Simple Random Sampling
◇ Stratified Sampling
◇ Cluster Sampling
◇ Systematic Sampling

- ◆ Non Probability Sampling
- ◇ Volunteer Sampling
- ◇ Haphazard Sampling

Some of the common data types are,

- ◆ Qualitative Data
- ◇ Binary Data
- ◇ Unordered Data
- ◇ Ordered Data

- ◆ Quantitative Data
- ◇ Continuous Data
- ◇ Discrete Data

Tabulate the data collected.

TO BE Data - Points to note

◆ Points to note while framing the TO BE Data

◇ Choose appropriate sampling mechanism – sample should be representative of population.
◇ Choose appropriate data type.
◇ Avoid fake data, actually collect the data.
◇ Most importantly, clearly mention what is collected.

TO BE Data - Example

◆ **TO BE Data:** Effort in minutes to fetch data and prepare report post automation (Mean) - 6.24 minutes

Reading No.	Effort in minutes to generate excel report
1	7
2	6
3	6
4	7
5	8
6	7
7	5
8	6
9	5
10	6
11	5
12	7
13	6
14	5
15	6
16	7
17	6
18	6
19	7
20	6
21	7
22	6
23	7
24	6
25	6

TO BE Process Capability - What and Why

◆ **What it is**

A concise description describing the capability of the improved process or product.

◆ **Why is it important**

This is an important component as it helps to understand the improved process or product performance capability.

TO BE Process Capability - How to Frame

◆ **Frame the TO BE Process Capability** with a view to answer the following questions,

◇ What is the capability or the sigma value of the improved process?

An online Sigma calculator can be used to calculate the process capability.

Following might be needed to calculate this,

◇ Mean
◇ Standard Deviation
◇ Specification Limits as defined by customer

TO BE Process Capability - Points to note

◆ Points to note while framing the TO BE Process Capability

◇ Ensure the right capability calculator is being used.

◇ Remember that Mean will be the mean of the TO BE collected data.

◇ Standard Deviation can be calculated for the collected data.

◇ Specification Limits can be calculated from goal statement target, or the CTQ performance requirements.

TO BE Process Capability - Example

◆ **TO BE Process Capability:**

◇ Mean - 6
◇ Standard Deviation - 0.77888809636986
◇ Specification Limits -
◇ LSL - 0
◇ USL - 24
◇ Potential Cp - 5.136
◇ Actual Cpk Index- 2.568

Data Review - What and Why

◆ **What it is**

A concise description describing the comparison of the performance of AS IS and TO BE process based on the collected data, preferably in a visually enhanced manner.

◆ **Why is it important**

This is an important component as it helps to evaluate the performance improvement achieved in the process as a result of the DMAIC project execution.

Data Review - How to Frame

◆ **Frame the Data Review** with a view to answer the following questions,

◇ What is the improvement achieved in the performance of the process, as a result of the DMAIC project execution?

To answer this, chart the data collected, for both AS IS and TO BE processes, side by side for a visually enhanced comparison and review.

Any of the following charts can be used,

◇ Bar Charts
◇ Column Charts
◇ Line Charts
◇ Pie Charts

However, the best charts for the purpose are the Pie and Bar Charts.

Data Review - Points to note

◆ Points to note while framing the Data Review

◇ Ensure the comparison is clear.
◇ Ensure the data is correctly charted without misplacement to avoid confusion.
◇ Choose clustered or stacked charts to bring out the difference in performance of the AS IS and TO BE processes effectively.

Data Review - Example

◆ **Data Review:**
◇ ASIS Effort - 120 minutes
◇ TOBE Effort - 6.24 minutes
◇ Effort Reduction Achieved - 113.76 min i.e. 94.8%

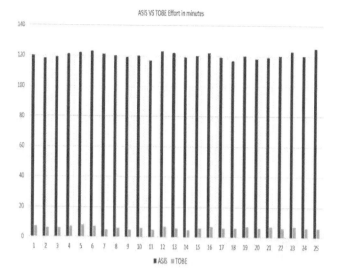
ASIS VS TOBE Effort in minutes

Monitor and Control Plan - What and Why

◆ **What it is**

A concise description describing the plan to monitor and control the improved process once it goes live.

◆ **Why is it important**

This is an important component as it helps to keep the solution working well and sustained post the DMAIC project execution.

Monitor and Control Plan - How to Frame

◆ **Frame the Monitor and Control Plan** with a view to answer the following questions,

◇ How will the improved process be used and by whom?

◇ How will the improved process be monitored post go live and by whom?

◇ What will be plan of action in case the improved process fails while live?

Monitor and Control Plan - Points to note

◆ Points to note while framing the Monitor and Control Plan

◇ Document the SOP correctly, Flow charts can also be used.

◇ Measures, and Specification limits should be defined by the customer.

◇ Do not ignore this, as this will be used to keep the improved process in control.

Monitor and Control Plan - Example

◆ Monitor and Control Plan:

Work Plan	Monitor Plan			Control Plan	
SOP	Key Measures	Target and Tolerance	Data Collection	Immediate Control	Process Improvement
1)Generate the automated report. 2)Email the report to Business Lead.	Number of times report was not generated as expected in a week.	Number of times report was not generated as expected in a week should be 0 with a USL of 1 time.	Check if the report is generated and record if not.	Manually create the report and send to the Business Lead.	Do RCA, fix the issue.

Realization Communication Signoff - What and Why

◆ What it is

A concise description clearly describing the calculation and summary of the cost and other savings and improvements as a result of executing the DMAIC project, along with the necessary hand over of the solution, and the Signoff from the sponsor for successful closure of the project.

◆ Why is it important

This is an important component as it helps to understand the benefits and improvements achieved as a result of the DMAIC project execution and to successfully close the project.

Realization Communication Signoff - How to Frame

◆ **Frame the Realization Communication Signoff** with a view to answer the following questions,

◇ Are the Hand Over formalities completed?
◇ What are the financial benefits achieved as a result of executing the DMAIC project?
◇ What are the Performance Improvements achieved as a result of executing the DMAIC project?
◇ What are the other benefits achieved as a result of executing the DMAIC project?

Calculate the costs incurred for the old and the new processes and mention the saving achieved.

Provide necessary training to the end users and maintenance teams on the new process or product.

Take formal signoff for the successful closure of the project from the sponsor.

Realization Communication Signoff - Points to note

◆ Points to note while framing the Realization Communication Signoff

◇ Ensure the calculations are accurate.
◇ The signoff is obtained from the sponsor to close the project.
◇ Also ensure proper training is given to the team who is going to use and maintain the new solution.

Realization Communication Signoff - Example

◆ **Realization Communication Signoff:**

◇ Before DMAIC effort - 120 minutes

◇ After DMAIC effort - 6 minutes

◇ Effort saved = 114 minutes (95%)

◇ Before DMAIC Costs: 120 minutes * 65 USD/hr * 365 days annually/ 60 minutes = 47450 USD

◇ After DMAIC Costs: 6 minutes * 65 USD/hr * 365 days annually/ 60 minutes = 2372.5 USD

◇ Annual Dollar Savings: 47450 - 2372.5 = 45077.5 USD

◇ Hand over -

◇ Knowledge Transfer conducted with the maintenance team.

◇ User Manuals shared with the end users.

◇ Sign off received from sponsor on 19th June 2018.

4 Blocker

This is the summary of the executed DMAIC project.

This covers all the important components of the entire DMAIC cycle like,

◇ Problem and Goal Statements.
◇ AS IS and TO BE Data Review.
◇ AS IS and TO BE Process Capability
◇ Realization and Signoff

Author's Note

I thank you for choosing the book, I have presented to you how exactly you can execute your Lean Six Sigma DMAIC projects with the most essential components.

I hope this adds value to you and helps you execute a good number of Lean Six Sigma DMAIC projects easily.

Please leave a review wherever you bought the book, and it will help me in my quest to provide good useful products to you on Lean Six Sigma.

All the very best,

Sumeet Savant
Lean Six Sigma Master Black Belt and Coach

Made in the USA
Coppell, TX
20 April 2022

76857684R00067